CHANGING OUTCOMES

*A Financial Recovery Strategy
for Peak-Career Physicians*

DAVID A. BURD CFP®
JAMES S. HEMPHILL CFP® CIMA

Text copyright © 2014

David A. Burd & James S. Hemphill

All Rights Reserved

ISBN-13: 978-1495201035

ISBN-10: 1495201031

Published By:
TGS Financial Advisors
170 N. Radnor Chester Rd.
Radnor, PA 19087

Table of Contents

Disclosure vii
Foreword ix
Introduction xi
About the Physician Profiles xiii
Physician Profile: Too Rich to Fail 3
The Bottomless Checkbook 5
Who Is Rich? 7
Where are the Doctors' Retirements? 9
The Illusion of Affluence 11
The Cliff 13
The Years the Locusts Have Eaten 19
Functional Wealth 21
Physician Profile: The Doctor as Analyst 25
Rotten Brains, Lousy Investments 27
Physician Profile: The Real Estate Illusion 31
Mid-Course Correction 33
Physician Profile: "Hail Mary" Investing 35
Treatment Plan 39

Seven Strategies.................................... 41
    Strategy 1   Convert bad assets to good assets....... 43
    Strategy 2   Optimize savings...................... 45
    Strategy 3   Pay yourself first, and make it automatic............................. 49
    Strategy 4   Manage discretionary spending 51
    Strategy 5   Invest sensibly 55
    Strategy 6   Pray for rain 59
    Strategy 7   Make a gradual transition.............. 61

Taking Stock...................................... 65
Finding the Right Advisor.......................... 67
Negotiating with Yourself 69
Keeping Score 71
Working the Plan.................................. 75
Physician Profile: Second Acts 79
Your Bigger Future 81
A Life Well Lived.................................. 83
Afterword... 85
About the Authors 87

Disclosure

As physicians understand only too well, we live in a world of litigation and regulation. For this reason, and to protect you as a reader, we offer the following legal cautions:

David A. Burd, CFP® and James S. Hemphill, CFP® are Managing Directors of TGS Financial Advisors, an SEC-registered investment adviser located in Radnor Pennsylvania. They have written this book as an introduction to the financial challenges faced by peak-career physicians.

The intent of this book is to help you to understand the financial landscape, not to give you a detailed roadmap to your own individual destination. No reader should regard this book as the receipt of, or a substitute for, personalized advice from Mr. Burd, Mr. Hemphill, or from TGS Financial Advisors, or from any other financial professional.

Please remember that different types of investments involve varying degrees of risk. Therefore, it should not be assumed that the future performance of any specific investment, investment product, or investment strategy (including the investments and/or investment strategies referenced in this book), or any of the book's non-investment related content, will be profitable, prove successful, or be applicable to any individual's specific situation.

Should a reader have any questions about how to apply the principles in this book to his or her individual situation, the reader is encouraged to consult with the professional advisors of his or her choosing.

Foreword

I thought it was a heart attack. I'd had rapid heartbeat and fatigue for several days. My internist diagnosed it as anxiety and prescribed a beta blocker. At a business lunch the next day, I was overcome with nausea, left early and headed home, where I took a shower to try to relax. I got out and toweled off. By the time I reached the bedroom thirty feet away, I was pouring sweat. Something was really wrong.

My wife drove me to the emergency room. We walked in, I sat down, and she announced to the nurse, "My husband is having a heart attack."

Half the population that walks into a suburban emergency room thinks they are having heart attacks. Most are wrong. Still, they took me in quickly. Within minutes, a nurse was attaching a blood oxygen sensor to my finger. She took one look at the reading and began moving fast. "We're taking you back," she said.

They began drawing blood right away. The ER doc was right there. I gave him a list of five names, all cardiologists. "Call Mike first. If he isn't in the hospital, call Greg." And so on down the list.

Within ten minutes, the first name on the list, my friend and client Mike, was at my bedside. He is one of the top cardiologists in southern New Jersey. He took one look at my chart and asked, "Is this your first heart attack?"

Then the blood work began to come back. "Huh. That is strange," he said. "We're not seeing what we'd expect to see." They kept working through their list of questions, until they got to 'Have you traveled recently?' I told them I had, a cross-country flight to Arizona followed by a six-hour car ride.

"Do you have any pain in your legs?" asked Mike. I told him that my left ankle and calf had been hurting for several days. He picked up my leg and began to palpate the calf.

It was not a heart attack. It was a deep vein thrombosis, almost certainly formed during long hours of sitting in plane and automobile. And it had detached and migrated to my lungs, where it broke up into several hundred blood clots.

Because I knew those names, because Mike arrived so quickly, because I live minutes from one of the best hospitals in my region of the country, I benefited from a life-saving diagnosis. I did spend a week in intensive care, while my physicians debated whether to administer TPA on top of the heparin in my IV, and my family waited to see if I would live or die. (In the end, they did not administer the TPA, and I did not die.)

I talked to that same cardiologist at his daughter's bat mitzvah. Amid the noise and chaos of sixty teenagers dancing and shouting, he leaned over so I could hear him. "You know, Dave," he said, "today cost a lot of money. But I never worried about it. I know I can afford it. And I wouldn't be here if it wasn't for you."

"You don't have to thank me, Mike. If not for you, I wouldn't be here either. At all."

My relationships with doctors are the foundation of my financial advisory practice. They pay my mortgage, make my car payments, send me on vacation, and put my two kids through college.

They also saved my life. This book represents much of what I've learned about the finances of physicians over more than thirty years in practice. It is part of my way of giving back.

David A. Burd
Voorhees, New Jersey
Spring, 2014

Introduction

A year ago, David and I wrote a book about finances for young physicians, *Pay Yourself First*. The book was well-received and widely distributed. It became the basis for a new fee-based program, designed to change the financial trajectory of the lives of young doctors.

Recently, a doctor who was a reader on drafts of that first book, a good friend, made a comment we weren't expecting. He told me, "I loved the book, and I'm going to share it with our residents. But I have a question. I really didn't do most of the things in the book, like push savings and reduce debt, when I was starting out. I bought the house, the cars, took the vacations. I've eaten some great meals, traveled to some really cool places. But I don't think I'm going to have enough money to retire. Is there anything I can do?"

At that time, we did not have a satisfactory answer for him. The argument of *Pay Yourself First* highlights the importance of tilting away from consumption and toward savings early in a medical career. One of the book's key takeaways is the magic of compound interest, given enough time for wealth to accumulate.

But what about a successful doctor like my friend? He is at the peak of his career, with a national reputation for surgical excellence, smart and funny, married to his medical-school sweetheart, another successful physician, with three great kids. But they have under-saved for years. Now they find themselves within sight of retirement, and they are worried they may not have enough wealth to retire with security.

Could we design a program, as systematic and data-driven as that in our first book, to provide that peak-career physician couple with confidence they can change their financial outcomes?

David and I met with the director of outreach for our physician advisory practice to discuss how to respond to my friend's question. "You need to write another book," she said.

So we did, and you are holding it.

Jim Hemphill
Radnor, PA
Spring 2014

About the Physician Profiles…

To safeguard the confidentiality of our clients and friends, we have altered the specifics of each physician profile by combining different families, changing names, altering place of residence or sub-specialty, and so on, so that no doctor will recognize herself or a colleague in this text.

This book is factual. It accurately reflects the real-world choices and their consequences we have observed, working with physicians in our advisory practice over more than thirty years. Every story is true, but none of them are accurate; each example is fictional, but firmly grounded in the financial realities of the lives of successful physicians.

OBSERVATIONS

Physician Profile: Too Rich to Fail

A few years ago, I received a referral to a potential client family. It was a pair of doctors, both highly-paid specialists, in their early 40s. I met them at their home.

They lived in a 6,500 square foot house on a double lot. They owned four cars, including two Porsches, a Lexus SUV and a Mercedes convertible. Their joint income was well over $1 million per year.

As we began talking, it quickly became clear that they believed they were rich. Seriously rich. In fact, they weren't really persuaded that they needed a financial advisor at all. In their minds, they were too rich to fail.

But they were nice folks, and so they engaged with me in the planning conversation, if only to be polite. Over a two-hour meeting, I began to get a clearer picture of their finances. In addition to their big house in Philadelphia's wealthy Main Line suburbs, they had two vacation properties: a beachfront home at the Jersey Shore and a condo on a golf course in South Carolina. All three properties were mortgaged. Three of their four cars were leased.

After almost ten years in practice, with an annual income in seven figures, they had less than $700,000 in financial assets. I asked them a simple question: "If you had to stop working, how long could you keep all this going?"

The question surprised them. They had never thought about it in those terms before.

"Maybe two or three years," guessed the husband.

The wife shook her head. "Not that long," she said. "Maybe not even a year."

Now they were paying attention. To their credit, they were smart and realistic. Once they got clear on the need to save, after we gave them hard numbers on what they would need to accumulate, they really turned things around. Less than five years later, they have sold both the shore house and the golf course condo, their debt-service costs are less than 10% of their income, and they are saving aggressively each month. Their investment net worth is in excess of $2 million and growing quickly.

They no longer believe they are rich. But they are confident, as they should be, that they are *becoming* rich. We'll discuss the moving parts of their financial transformation later in the book. But first, let's try to understand what made them feel that they were too rich to fail.

—DAB

1   The Bottomless Checkbook

"I can't be broke. I still have checks left."
                              Spendthrift spouse

If you are like most of our physician clients, you have probably never bounced a check. You aren't spendthrift. You don't buy everything you see, but if you really want something—a new Range Rover, a vacation in Hawaii, a case of California cult Cabernet—you simply write a check or pull out your American Express card.

At any given time, you may easily have five or even six figures in your checking account. We call this "the bottomless checkbook," and it can easily lead to confusion between immediate liquidity and long-term financial security.

The typical American family has an early-warning system about financial distress: their checkbook is empty. They are sometimes in danger of running out of money before they run out of month. But most physicians reach retirement without ever taking a dinnertime phone call from a bill collector, missing a mortgage payment, or failing to pay off their credit card bills every month.

Blessed with more dollars in *liquid assets* than most Americans ever accumulate in *net worth*, it is easy for a successful physician to feel financially bulletproof. A physician can easily practice for thirty years without ever having a serious worry about money. Until he approaches retirement, and realizes he is desperately short of the capital he will need to preserve his lifestyle.

The unfortunate reality is that most physicians fail to accumulate enough wealth to fund a successful retirement. Your checkbook can't tell you whether you are over-spending and under-saving. You will need a different measure.

2   Who Is Rich?

"He is rich enough who owes nothing."

French proverb

Twenty years ago, researcher Tom Stanley turned our understanding of wealth upside down with his book, *The Millionaire Next Door*. Using hard data, he demonstrated that American millionaires are not who we think.

A relatively small number of millionaires are highly-paid professionals like doctors, dentists and lawyers. Most don't live in mansions and drive imported automobiles. They live in quite ordinary houses, often bought decades ago, with mortgages paid off, and they drive Fords. Disproportionately, they are business owners, often in blue-collar trades.

Here is a simple measure of how you are doing at building wealth, compared to others your age. *Take your pre-tax annual income, divide it by 10, and multiply it by your age.*

Here's an example. Let's assume you are a cardiologist earning $400,000 per year, fifteen years out of fellowship, age 50. This yields the following formula:

$$\frac{\$400,000}{10} \times 50 = \$2,000,000$$

This formula provides us with a baseline measure of capital accumulation.[1] Using this measure, how do physicians perform at building wealth?

In his second book, *The Millionaire Mind*, Stanley offers the following table, which compares the accumulation of assets across high-income groups:

High-Income-Producing Occupational Groups
Percentage Who Are Superior Wealth Accumulators

Stockbrokers	Physicians	Lawyers	Corporate Executives	Business Owners
13.6%	21.8%	29.0%	43.3%	46.3%

---

[1] This formula provides a quick, back-of-the-envelope measure of wealth accumulation. It should not be confused with a your own unique, calculated and personal retirement accumulation target. Depending on the specifics of your situation and intentions, you will probably need two to five times that number at retirement.

8   Changing Outcomes

As you can see, doctors and stockbrokers perform poorly, lawyers somewhere in the middle, while executives and business owners are more likely to accumulate significant wealth per dollar of income.

Why do doctors under-perform at building wealth? For the same reason stockbrokers are even *less* successful at getting rich than doctors—the confusion of consumption, status, and wealth.

Who is richer? The physician who drives a Lexus, lives in a 5,000 square foot house, and vacations in the California wine country, who has $500,000 in her 401k plan and $100,000 in her bank account? Or the electrical contractor who drives a pickup truck with 200,000 miles on it, lives in a 2,800 square foot home with a paid-off mortgage, and has investment assets of $2 million?

In our advisory practice, we use the following practical definition of wealth. *You are rich when you can maintain your chosen lifestyle, for as long as you live, without being required to work.*

Notice three things about our definition:

➤ In *choosing* your desired lifestyle, you determine the assets you will need to accumulate.

➤ You are not required to retire when you hit your wealth goal, unless you wish.

➤ Assets that don't produce an economic return, no matter how costly, can't support your lifestyle. (More on this later.)

The physicians we work with find this a useful and practical measure of wealth. They like the idea of being financially independent, in a very practical, real-world sense. Their goal is to reach the position where continuing their medical career is no longer an economic necessity, but simply one option among many. With finances secure, their question is how to lead the most engaged and fulfilling life possible. (Very often, their answer is to continue to practice medicine.)

In a perfect world, all physicians would have the wealth they need to make optimal choices. Unfortunately, this is not a perfect world, and most peak-career doctors fall far short of accumulating walk-away wealth.

3 Where are the Doctors' Retirements?

"Where Are the Customers' Yachts?"

Fred Schwed Jr.

Back in the 1960s, Fred Schwed wrote a book about who really gets rich on Wall Street, pointing out that it is the brokers who own the yachts, not their clients.

So why do those clients keep coming back, making their brokers richer than they are? The answer is surprising. Many investors, in choosing a financial advisor, prefer one who they perceive to be *financially more successful* than themselves. Their measure of an advisor's success? What he wears, what car he drives, and where he lives.

This illustrates a larger principle. For many affluent Americans, living large is the visible proof of success. This is not evidence of a national character flaw. In fact, it is simply an aspect of our innate social psychology.

Human beings are primates, not squirrels. We are hard-wired to pay more attention to our status within the tribe than to storing up acorns for the winter. Psychologists call the process of evaluating your status against your peers *social comparison*. The higher a person's non-economic status, the stronger the drive becomes to make their material status conform. Since physicians have higher reputational status than other professions, they are bombarded with spending cues.

Doctors respond to the same social cues as other high-income individuals. At a level below conscious choice, many doctors believe a key measure of their success is the material wealth they display. Historically, few professions devote as large a share of income toward personal consumption as physicians.

You probably have physician friends or colleagues who live in magnificent houses, drive luxury cars, own sailboats, start wineries or open restaurants. Some even buy yachts.[2]

Status cues are present in every human society. Where you live, what you drive, what you wear, what your children wear, how much you give to charity, whether your children attend public or private schools, what colleges you

---

[2]Several physicians have told us that they see a watershed between doctors trained before the 1980s and those trained afterwards. The former group, who began practice when medical incomes were rising sharply, was much more likely to pursue high-status lifestyles. For younger doctors, today the pursuit of status takes an absolute back seat to the struggle for medical autonomy, and financial independence often seems more of a wish than a tangible and realistic goal.

10 Changing Outcomes

aspire to for them, even the news sources you follow: all provide powerful information about status.

The failure of most doctors to build enough wealth isn't due to some unique character flaw. It simply reflects American society's preference for consumption over savings, and the desire of competitive, hard-working individuals to dominate status hierarchies.

If you are a doctor age 50 or above and have saved only a fraction of what you will need to enjoy a secure retirement, there is a highly technical term that applies to you—you are a *typical American*. Your savings deficit does not make you exceptional. What you may have trouble accepting is your *failure* to be exceptional, in the context of your lifetime of achievement.

4   The Illusion of Affluence

Doing the research for our first book, which was aimed at doctors beginning practice, helped us to understand the forbidding economics of medicine at the outset of a doctor's career. In 2013, a typical new physician started practice with over $175,000 in education debt. That new doctor's higher income is partly an illusion, because it ignores the practical necessity of paying off medical school debts whose interest is not tax-deductible, with earned income taxed at a Federal marginal tax rate as high as 39.6%.

A similar tension between perception and financial reality exists toward the end of a doctor's career. To illustrate, let's compare the finances of a retiring public school teacher with those of a cardiologist at the same age:

	Teacher	Physician
Working:		
Income	$70,000	$350,000
Marginal tax bracket	15%	33%
At retirement:		
Retirement savings	$250,000	$1,000,000
Pension	$35,000	$0
Social Security	$24,200	$30,000
Total scheduled income	$59,200	$30,000
Income replacement ratio	*84%*	*8%*

The teacher retires with only $250,000 in investments, in addition to which he will receive both a pension and a Social Security benefit. He might not need to withdraw *anything* from his portfolio to duplicate the after-tax cash flow he received while working.

Contrast this with a cardiac surgeon with $1 million of investments at retirement. After a lifetime of work she has accumulated assets equal to only three or four years of spending. In terms of the funds needed to sustain her lifestyle in retirement, this is a disastrous shortfall.

Yet compared to most Americans, she is rich. Really rich. In fact, having net worth of $1 million places her in the top 3% of all Americans. If we assume she also owns a home and other non-financial assets, she's richer still.

12 Changing Outcomes

Let's assume that physician, with $1 million in productive assets, can expect a Social Security benefit of $2,900 per month ($35,000 per year) at age 67. This will replace less than 10% of her pre-tax income during her working years, while the combination of pension and Social Security will replace more than 80% of working income for the schoolteacher.

Especially as they approach the retirement transition, the perception of "rich doctor" versus "middle-class teacher" is economically backwards. It is the teacher, not the physician, who is financially equipped to maintain his lifestyle; it will be the physician, not the teacher, who must curtail her spending sharply in retirement.

Our point is simple. At the end of their careers, as at the beginning, much of the apparent wealth of doctors is an illusion. *Don't let the illusion of wealth distract you from building the real wealth you will need to live the life you want for decades after you retire.*

5   The Cliff

The financial consequences of under-accumulation can be illustrated visually. If you arrive at retirement without enough investment assets to sustain your pre-retirement spending level, you have two choices:

1) Reduce your spending to what you can sustain long-term.

2) Keep spending as you have been, and run entirely out of assets in a relatively short time. For the rest of your life, live on a fraction of the cash flow you spent during your working years.

This chart illustrates the first strategy. The gap between the spending level during the working years, and that sustainable in retirement, we refer to as *The Cliff*.

The Cliff™

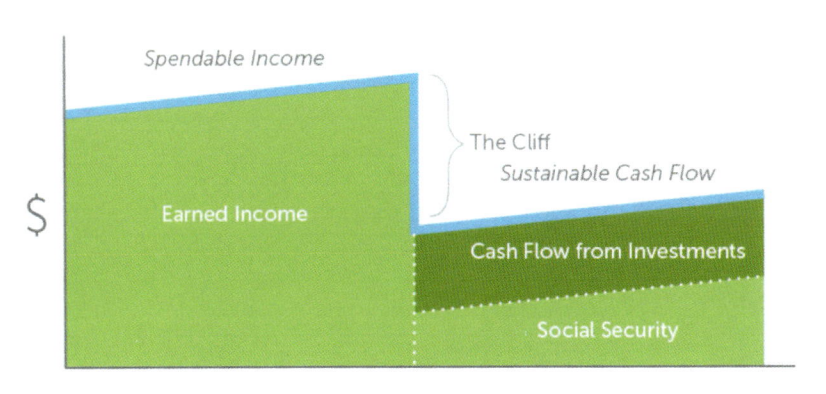

Spendable Income

The Cliff
Sustainable Cash Flow

Earned Income

Cash Flow from Investments

Social Security

Pre-Retirement Post-Retirement

14 Changing Outcomes

The graphic above illustrates the fact pattern of a well-informed and self-disciplined individual, who upon retirement immediately cuts back his spending to a level sustainable for the rest of his life. As shown in the graphic below, capital may gradually be drawn down, but it is never exhausted.[3]

Sustainable Retirement Cash Flow

Capital

$

Cash Flow from Investments

Social Security Payments

Time

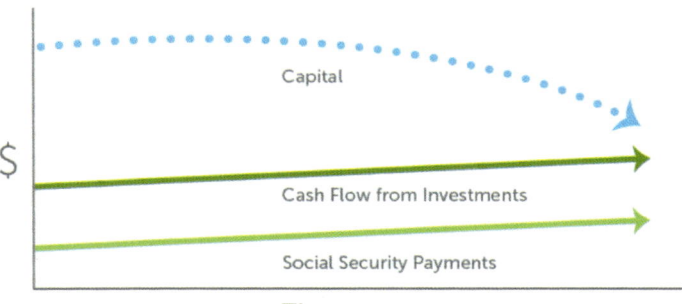

Unfortunately, most retirees with savings don't immediately reduce their spending. Instead, they struggle to keep up their pre-retirement lifestyle for as long as possible. Once they exhaust their savings, they hit an even more severe *Cliff*, as shown below. (Note that spending is initially *higher* than in the sustainable scenario, but sharply *lower* once capital is exhausted.)

Unsustainable Retirement Cash Flow

Capital

$

Cash Flow from Investments

The Cliff

Social Security Payments

Capital is exhausted

Time

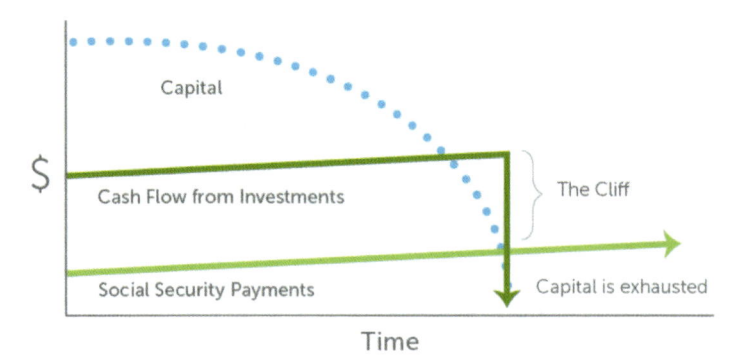

[3]Note that we depict income going up, both before and after retirement. This is meant to illustrate the long-term problem of inflation, which is likely to increase a retiree's cost of living substantially over time. The actual inflation rate today is much lower than the slope of the line in the graphic suggests.

Understanding *The Cliff* is a first step toward clearer thinking about your own lifetime financial security. The strategies in this book are designed to do one thing—*make your personal Cliff as shallow as possible at retirement.*

As you commit a larger portion of your pre-retirement income to savings, you build your net worth. This increases your sustainable post-retirement cash flow, and *The Cliff* grows smaller. Instead of an abrupt and painful change of state, our aim is to help you create a more gradual step-function—a moderate reduction in lifestyle at age 55, followed by another moderate reduction at retirement, rather than a permanent, catastrophic fall in income at age 75.

DIAGNOSIS

6   The Years the Locusts Have Eaten

"The perfect is the enemy of the good."
                                  Voltaire

Here's a table from our first book, illustrating two saving/spending sequences:

- ➤ Save 20% of your income starting at age 35, continue through age 45, and then stop. (Ten years of savings.)
- ➤ Spend your income when you begin practice at age 35, then start saving aggressively at age 45, putting away 20% of income, and continue through retirement at age 65. (Twenty years of savings.)

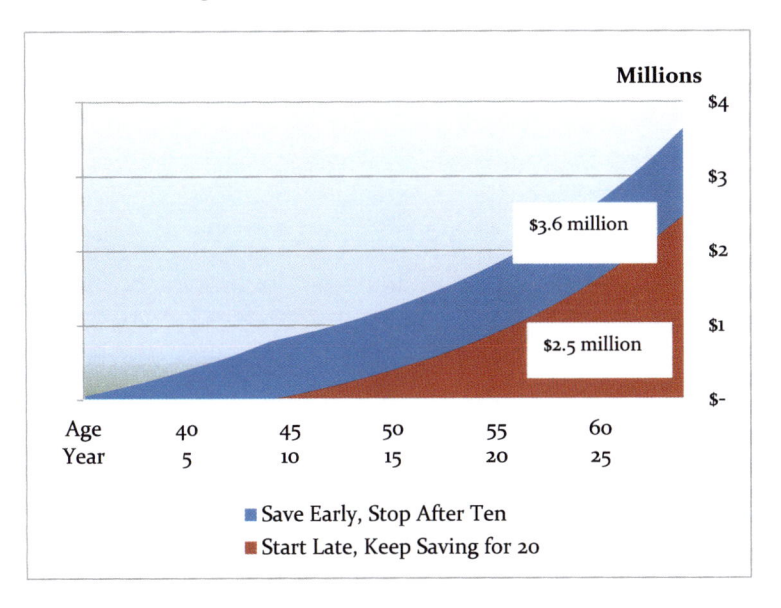

Changing Outcomes

Here's the same data set in table form:[4]

	Save Early, Stop After Ten	**Start Late, Keep Saving for 20**
Total Savings	$500,000	$1,000,000
Total Earnings	$3,146,147	$1,471,146
Ending Value	$3,646,147	$2,471,146
Savings % of Total	13.7%	40.5%

As you can see, the late saver does not ever catch up to the early saver, despite saving for twice as long and putting aside twice as many dollars out of income. *Almost 90% of the early saver's total wealth comes from earnings—from the compounding effect of money-making money—while less than 60% of the late saver's wealth comes from compounding.*

This demonstrates the magic—and tyranny—of compound interest. If you fail to start saving early and with intention, you may never be able to fully catch up, even if you push very hard later in your career.

We are not sharing this information to make you depressed. Few Americans save enough to fund a secure retirement. But we do intend to make clear the urgency of acting *now*, before any more time passes.

If you are in your fifties, your goal isn't to catch up to that rare colleague who began saving with intention the moment he began practice, as long as ten, fifteen or even twenty years ago. Your goal should be practical and personal—*improve your financial position, for the rest of your life, starting right now.*

---

[4] In both the graph and the table, we are assuming gross income of $250,000, savings of $50,000 per year, and investment returns of 8% per year.

7 Functional Wealth

"You got to get your mind right."

Boss Paul
Cool Hand Luke

One of the hottest areas of medicine right now is functional aging. According to this model, your *chronological* age is less important than your *functional* age, as defined by your mental and physical state.

You need not buy into the more extreme projections of the life extension crowd to recognize medical science's improving ability to help individuals maintain a high degree of physical function as they age.[5] These days, Americans in their 70s, 80s, even 90s are competing in weightlifting events, cycling cross country, skiing double-black-diamond trails, and climbing mountains. *Focusing on function rather than chronological age helps people live better even as they grow older.*

We propose a similar emphasis on functionality as it applies to your wealth.

Our view is very different from the standard approach to personal finances. If you ask an accountant to prepare a net worth statement, he will list your assets and your liabilities, and deduct the latter from the former in order to determine your net worth. An example of such a balance sheet is on the next page.

A successful physician couple in their 50s, with joint income in the mid six figures, might look at this balance sheet and conclude all is well. They are millionaires, in fact, almost multi-millionaires.

---

[5] Recently, I spent two days at a seminar with Ray Kurzweil, author of *The Singularity is Near* and now Director of Engineering for Google's artificial intelligence effort. He believes that, if you can stay alive for the next two decades, science will learn how to arrest the aging process. -JSH

Balance Sheet of Jane & John Medico

Assets		
	Checking accounts	$100,000
	Certificates of Deposit	$25,000
	401k plans	$450,000
	Principal residence	$825,000
	Vacation property	$1,250,000
	Time share condo	$50,000
	Automobiles	$100,000
	Personal property	$250,000
	Artwork	$150,000
Total assets:		$3,200,000
Liabilities		
	Mortgage on principal residence	$550,000
	Mortgage on vacation property	$900,000
	Auto loans	$60,000
	Credit cards	$10,000
Total liabilities:		$1,520,000
Net worth		$1,680,000

What's the problem with this picture? *Almost everything in the assets column costs money every month.* Much of it (cars and personal property) loses value from the day it is purchased. The *only* assets these doctors own that will put money in their pockets over time are the investment assets.

Here is a revised net worth statement, showing only *functional assets*, which we define as those with predictable positive cash flows over time. (We still show all liabilities, since these continue to take money out of pocket each month.)

Functional Balance Sheet of Jane & John Medico[6]

Functional assets		
	Checking accounts	$100,000
	Certificates of Deposit	$25,000
	401k plans	$450,000
Total functional assets:		*$575,000*
Liabilities		
	Auto Loans	$60,000
	Credit Cards	$10,000
	Mortgage on principal residence	$550,000
	Mortgage on vacation property	$900,000
Total liabilities:		*$1,520,000*
Functional net worth		*-$945,000*

A very different picture, isn't it?

The functional balance sheet shows how much money you have working for you. As you can see, these two hard-working, capable and successful physicians are working to support their lifestyle assets, rather than having assets that work for them.

To paraphrase President Kennedy, "Ask not what you can do for your assets. Ask what your assets can do for you." *When you think about your net worth, remember that only investment assets count.*

Later in this book, we'll provide a strategy for re-engineering your balance sheet over as little as five years, so you can begin to multiply the rate at which you build your functional net worth.

---

[6] We do not include the principal residence in this net worth statement, even though a residence is a necessity of life. Our experience is that the biggest obstacle to financial security for many Americans is the size and expense of their home. The best way to think about your home is as an expensive and durable consumer good, not much different from an automobile or a refrigerator. The larger the home, the higher the associated expenses, and the harder it will be to build functional wealth.

Physician Profile: The Doctor as Analyst

"I think I would rather be doing your job."

Physician to financial advisor
End of tech stock bubble, 1999

We have all seen the commercials. The E-Trade baby with his golf game and his limo driver. The Scottrade investor whose software understands his unique trading style. We are living in a time when millions of people think that short-term stock trading (or worse, trading commodities, options or currencies) is a rational use of their time.

Some of those day traders are doctors. Pretty much all of them are wasting their time, and far too many are compromising their financial security.

An old friend of mine is an extremely able physician. He once made an over-the-phone diagnosis, quickly confirmed by examination, which may have saved the sight in one of my eyes. For years, he has been an active amateur investor, researching, buying, and selling a variety of different securities.

What is the expected return on all of his work and study? *Zero. Nada. Zilch.*

He is studying the same stocks as literally thousands of other amateur and professional analysts. Every trade he makes has an equally well-motivated and often better-capitalized investor on the other side. And none of those traders will gain an advantage unless they have a unique insight at odds with the consensus of all the other analysts. *The price of any publicly-traded company already reflects the self-interested assessments of thousands, tens of thousands, maybe even millions of different individuals and institutions.*

If you are an investor in tech stocks, you might know Apple's market share in world smartphone markets and their return on equity to two decimal places, but that knowledge won't make you a penny more from owning the stock than someone who chose it by throwing a dart at *The Wall Street Journal*.

Professional investors expect known information about any company to already be 'priced in' to its stock. If the company is going gangbusters, that is already priced in. If the company's flagship product just hit an iceberg, that is priced in as well. This concept, the idea that all public information is already reflected in the price of all publicly-traded securities, is known as *efficient markets theory*.

The reality of market efficiency is particularly difficult for physician-investors to accept, since their lifetime experience is that study and hard work are the *cause* of their success.

But even if you think you possess the right stuff to be a superior investor, it is probably not worth your time to find out. A typical doctor works 50 hours or more each week. He already has less free time than most people. Let's assume he has been in practice for ten to fifteen years, and has built up $500,000 in common stock investments, in addition to the mutual funds in his 401k. Why not manage that stock portfolio himself, save an advisor's fees, and improve his returns?

Let's run the numbers. If he spends five hours a week on his investments, that adds up to 250 hours a year. Let's assume his research and active management work out, and he beats the markets, net of fees and costs, by 2% per year. (Not bloody likely, say the data, but let's proceed.)

He has made a profit from his investment skill of $10,000. So for each of his 250 hours of work, he's earned $40. Not much more than a waiter takes home after a busy Friday night at T. G. I. Friday's. And this assumes he finds the persistent return advantage most professional investors fail to realize, instead of the large disadvantages experienced by most individual investors.

Many doctors turn to active management of their investment portfolios in order to recover a sense of control over their finances: "I'm not ignoring my financial future. I'm buying and selling, researching companies, looking for opportunities."

But if all of that activity has no predictable economic benefit, it is a distraction, not a solution. Don't let being an investment hobbyist prevent you from coming to grips with the real drivers of your lifetime financial security.

8   Rotten Brains, Lousy Investments

> *"He's got a rotten brain! It's rotten, I tell you, rotten!"*
> Gene Wilder
> Mel Brooks' Young Frankenstein

So far we have focused on the tension between saving and spending. Now we need to focus on another important factor that holds doctors back from building walk-away wealth.

Doctors are lousy investors. That may sound harsh, but thirty years in practice tells us it is generally true. You can probably think of several colleagues who have made spectacularly bad investment decisions.

Physicians are not alone in making sub-optimal investment decisions. Consider this data on mutual fund investor performance from research firm DALBAR, for the twenty-year period ending December 31, 2013:[7]

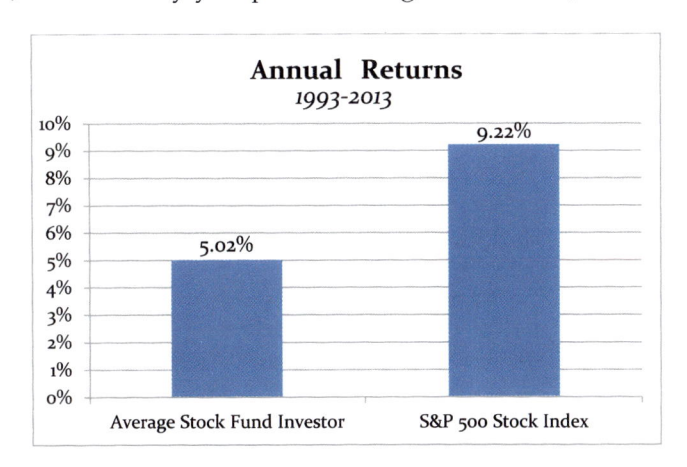

Annual Returns
1993-2013

Average Stock Fund Investor	5.02%
S&P 500 Stock Index	9.22%

Understand what these data mean—it is not that the typical mutual *fund* underperformed the market by 45%. It is that the typical *investor* in mutual funds underperformed—by choosing the wrong funds, by being in or out of the market at the wrong times, by chasing performance in up markets and panicking during down markets—in short, by trying to do *better* than the markets, investors did much *worse*.

---

[7]*DALBAR Quantitative Analysis of Investor Behavior 2014.*

28   Changing Outcomes

The emerging discipline of behavioral economics documents a consistent pattern of investment decision-making mistakes among almost all investors, caused by a combination of over-confidence, behavioral errors, and lack of skill. The result is long-term investment results that are at least one-third lower than those of the financial markets, which are available to anyone simply by owning an index fund.

Neither smarts nor study will save you. The fact that you graduated near the top of your medical school class won't prevent you from being greedy or fearful, nor will it cure you of confirmation bias, framing effects or attribution errors. Poor investment outcomes are not the result of *cognitive* deficits, nor do they reflect *informational* disadvantages. They result from powerful, persistent and intrinsic *behavioral* biases.[8]

Consider one central insight of behavioral economics: *Most individuals are over-confident about almost everything, almost all the time.* In general, over-confidence is a survival trait. Who would have asked their future spouse out on a date, cultivated a potato, eaten an oyster, crossed the oceans to the New World, written a first novel, or signed up to take the MCATs, without healthy self-confidence?

Unfortunately, over-confidence can be deadly for investors. Long-term investment success requires a disciplined understanding of what we *can* and *cannot* predict; in a sense, being a successful investor requires a specific, rational *lack of confidence.*

Yet if there is one essential characteristic of most physicians, it is self-confidence. This is particularly true of surgical specialists. If you are poised above someone's left ventricle, scalpel in hand, you had better not be paralyzed by self-doubt.

That sort of robust confidence simply isn't an asset for an investor. Successful investing requires both a different technical skill set and a different psychological makeup from those that make you successful as a physician.[9]

If you already recognize that your investment results have been poor or inconsistent, we will offer several simple, sensible investment strategies later in this book. But perhaps you consider yourself a successful investor. If so, ask

---

[8]In fact, some data on identical twins raised in separate households appears to demonstrate that investment success is largely based on innate psychological traits, not on experience or training. (In other words, Warren Buffett was born, not made.)

[9]Some psychological research suggests that *everyone* is systematically and consistently over-confident...except for those suffering from clinical depression, who are able to assess their own abilities very accurately. So you might want to be sure your investment advisor has a scrip for Zoloft.

yourself this question: *How have my investment results compared to a passive index strategy, on a risk-adjusted basis, for the last one, three, five and ten years?*

You probably don't have a good answer to that question. In our experience, few individual investors, over the more than twenty years we've run our independent advisory practice, have been able to answer that question accurately. The few who believed they knew the answer were usually wildly incorrect.

As a physician, you would never implement a medical procedure without the evidence that it would improve outcomes for your patients. Yet most physician-investors invest for a lifetime without ever comparing their own results to any objective metric.

Physician Profile: The Real Estate Illusion

"I'm putting my money in something I can touch—real estate. They can't take that away from me."

Florida real estate buyer[10]
June 2006

It is time to focus on the "investment" asset that has done more damage to the financial security of physicians than any other—real estate.

One of our earliest physician clients was an internist from suburban Philadelphia. Shortly before we met, he bought a condo in Phoenix, right at the peak of the Sunbelt real estate bubble of the late 1970s. He was underwater pretty much from the day he settled. The interest rate on his mortgage was over 10% and his payments over $1,000 per month, back when $1,000 would really buy something. He neither used the condo nor rented it.

When we first became aware of this investment, and understood the numbers, we advised him to sell it and take the loss. He refused, sharing a characteristic sentiment: "I can't afford to take a $40,000 loss. Besides, my brother might want to retire there. Or maybe Martha and I will move there when I retire."

Even as interest rates fell in the mid-1980s, he could not re-finance his mortgage. Since he had negative equity in the property, the remaining mortgage principal was higher than the market value, and banks back then did not lend without collateral. (These days, we call this being "upside down.") We suggested he re-finance his primary residence instead, and use the proceeds to retire the high-rate debt on the condo. Again, he declined. He had worked hard to pay off his mortgage early, and would not consider having any debt on his home—even if the practical consequence was paying much higher interest costs on a property far away.

By the early 1990s, he had paid down enough principal that he was no longer underwater. Again, we advised him to sell. He refused. You can guess

---

[10] The individual who shared this nugget of wisdom was not a physician. Unfortunately, he was wrong about real estate, at least real estate that is mortgaged. Over four years, he built a substantial Florida real estate portfolio, all mortgaged, most of it producing no net cash flow. When the crash hit, and his business income dropped, he could no longer pay the monthly mortgage bills. The banks did, in fact, take it all away from him, one property at a time, through the unpleasant process of foreclosure.

how this story ends. He never re-financed, never rented. He did not retire to Phoenix, where he had no family, but to the Washington DC suburbs, where his children lived.

Eventually, after twenty years, the property was paid off. (For five years, he double-paid the principal on the mortgage rather than fully funding his retirement plan.) When he retired from independent practice and went to work for the hospital, he finally sold the Phoenix property, more than twenty years after he bought it, for a price equal to his original purchase price (ignoring the loss in real value caused by two decades of inflation).

Over that period, he had paid over $200,000 in debt service. This was during the heart of the greatest bull market in human history, when $10,000 invested in the S&P 500 Stock Index at the end of July 1982 grew to more than $235,000 by the end of 1999. Had he committed that same monthly cash flow to a dollar-cost-averaging purchase of the Vanguard Index 500 mutual fund, it might easily have been worth over $2,000,000, an amount that would have tripled his functional net worth at retirement.

A single bad investment, made with borrowed money and held doggedly for decades, waiting for the price to recover, fundamentally compromised his financial security.

The point of this story is *not* that stocks are always a better investment than real estate. You can make serious money, or lose serious money, in either stocks or property. The financial crisis of 2008-2009, which was triggered by the sharp drop in residential real estate values and followed by the worst bear market in U. S. stocks since 1929, conclusively demonstrates the risks of both real estate and stocks.

There are two key takeaways here:

➢ There is no special magic to real estate.[11]

➢ Almost always, the best thing to do with a losing investment is to get out.

---

[11] One of the doctors we consulted on this book asked for clarification on a specific aspect of real estate investing. "I own the building where my practice is located. Surely that is a good investment?" Our answer is that it depends on the price paid for the building, in relation to the rental income stream net of costs. Bought at a good (low) price, a medical office building might be a fine investment, regardless of whether your own practice was domiciled within that property. Conversely, bought at a bad (high) price, a medical building would be a bad investment, whether or not you were paying rent to yourself. With real estate as with any other investment, you must ignore the clichés and *run the numbers*.

9 Mid-Course Correction

"We are all suffering from a chronic, sexually-transmitted condition with a 100% mortality rate. It is called life."

Pediatric surgeon
Mid-Atlantic

By now, we hope you are convinced of three things:

1) Most Americans, including most doctors, are the unwitting victims of a consumption-based measure of success that leads to chronic over-spending and under-saving.

2) If you are a typical physician at the peak of your career, you have probably accumulated less than half of the wealth you will need to maintain your standard of living in retirement.

3) Most investors, due to intrinsic behavioral biases, make sub-optimal investment decisions, and earn returns significantly below those available in the financial markets. Physicians as a group are poor investors.

If you are able to recognize yourself in this picture, it is time to move on from problems toward solutions. There is absolutely no point in beating yourself up for having responded to our society's ever-present pro-spending social cues, especially if you lacked a robust measure of an alternative model of success. Nor is there any point in re-visiting past investment errors.

But regrets entirely aside, if you are like most peak-career physicians, you are nowhere near where you need to be financially. The next section will offer a concrete strategy designed to get you back on track.

Physician Profile: "Hail Mary" Investing

Recently I attended my 35th college reunion. It was fun to catch up with old friends, and fascinating to observe who seemed unchanged, who was changed beyond recognition, and who I simply didn't remember, even out of a small class of 300.

One of the folks I talked to was an old classmate, Johnny. He is a plastic surgeon with a successful practice. He knows what I do for a living, and without much prompting, he started telling me about his investments.

He understands that he is behind the curve on accumulation, and he is trying to make it up. But he is not buying quality securities, or making regular dollar-cost-averaging contributions to a mutual fund. Instead, he recently put all of his non-retirement investment funds into a new-construction apartment deal.

This is a classic late-career investment error. Johnny is trying to make up for a lifetime of under-accumulation by hitting one investment home run. This almost never works. Whether the get-rich-quick deal involves buying apartments, chasing precious metals, or committing funds to any other high-risk scheme, trying to make up all at once for a lifetime of under-saving and bad investment decisions is rarely a winning strategy.

Since Johnny was a star football player, I'll offer a sports analogy. Picture your preparation for retirement as a football game. If you are age 50 or older, you are already well into the second half. The game isn't over, but the clock is surely ticking. If you are short on retirement savings, it is like being down by 17 points midway through the third quarter. With more than twenty minutes on the clock, you need three scores to win the game. Assume your passing game stinks, but your running game is solid. What should you do?

Play good defense, keep the other guys from putting more points on the board, and run the football. In investment terms, avoid new debts, don't make any investments that could end in a total loss, push savings, and own quality assets with growth potential.

You can't try to get it all back on one big play. No Hail Mary passes into traffic. No high-risk, high-return speculations. No hedge funds, apartment deals, or commodity trading partnerships. No leveraged investments in gold, Bitcoins or baseball cards.

Here's the good news. *You don't need to win the game.* You may not accumulate enough assets to preserve your existing lifestyle, dollar-for-dollar, from the day you retire until the end of your life, decades from now. (Again, few Americans do.) But you can dramatically improve your prospective outcome,

35

compared to how well you are doing now without a plan; *you can beat the point spread*.

In a society where almost everyone under-saves for retirement, that is actually a very big win.

—JSH

TREATMENT

10 Treatment Plan

"As physicians, we have all come to accept one basic fact. We can't stop Americans from dying."

> Oregon physician
> Quoted on Sixty Minutes

When we began to wrestle with the issue of the peak-career physician who has under-saved for retirement, we struggled with what to offer. We've dealt with successful doctors for decades, but most of our clients have been lifetime high savers, and have been in the top quintile of physician net worth since their early years in practice.

The strategies we offered for young doctors in our first book would not solve the problems of older doctors. A doctor in his fifties may have higher income than his younger associate, and does not face the expense of starting up a household, but he lacks one crucial advantage—*time*.

Our breakthrough came in a conversation with a physician friend who has since become a client. He told us, "I'm not looking for a miracle. I'm looking for a *strategy*."

Doctors don't expect perfect results. No matter how skilled, no physician can keep his patients alive forever. In medicine, there are no final victories, but there can be countless battles won—improvements in quality of life both small and large; better outcomes whether measured by extra years lived, pain relieved, or function restored.

Imagine you had a new patient, a male in his 50s, fifty pounds overweight, with cholesterol off the charts. Would you tell him, "I'm sorry, you should have started exercising and reducing saturated fats twenty years ago. I can't help you now," or would you prescribe statins, counsel him on healthy weight loss, and monitor his lipids closely?

Do you abandon him because he is an imperfect patient, or work tirelessly to help him to improve his outcomes? We know what our physicians do—they treat their patients as effectively as they can.

Our job is similar.

As middle-aged fat guys, we've sat across the desk from many doctors, usually as advisors but plenty of times as patients. Our job is not to rescue our friends, our healers, our doctors. Our job is to do exactly what they do every day for their patients, who are themselves imperfect human beings—not perform miracles, but *improve outcomes*, by applying the best tools and techniques available.

11   Seven Strategies

"Put the big rocks in first."

Chemistry professor to
freshman students[12]

We have tried to avoid the temptation to make this book into a "brain transfer" that communicates everything we have learned about personal finance in more than thirty years in practice. Instead, we are focused on a few key moving parts. Here are the seven strategies we believe have the greatest power to drive a late-career financial recovery:

1) Convert bad assets to good assets.
2) Optimize risk-adjusted after-tax savings.
3) Pay yourself first, and make it automatic.
4) Manage discretionary spending.
5) Invest sensibly.
6) Pray for rain.
7) Make a gradual transition.

Every strategy here will not have application to every physician. We suggest that you read this section carefully, and identify the specific strategies that will offer *you* the most advantages. *Put the big rocks in first.*

---

[12] If you don't recognize this punchline to a very old story, send us an email and we will explain it.

Strategy 1   Convert bad assets to good assets

We have found that decisions about unproductive assets are a key measure of whether a financial turnaround will succeed. If you are not willing to unload that 12-metre racing sailboat and turn the capital to more productive uses, your financial recovery is unlikely to succeed.

Remember the high-income physician couple from the first chapter, who owned three expensive properties, but had less than a year's income in functional assets? For tax purposes, they treated both vacation properties as investments, which meant they could use each for a maximum of ten days a year. They got to their shore house off-season, but rarely even visited the golf course condo. Both properties were rented during peak seasons, but the shore house never rented except during the summer, and the golf course condo was often empty. Neither property came close to covering its costs from rental income.

One of our first recommendations was that they sell the vacation home and the golf course condo. They were very resistant at first, but we pushed hard, and they eventually came around and sold both properties.

Months later, we were scheduled for our annual review meeting with them, and we worried they might have lingering resentment over how hard we had pushed them to sell. We could not have been more wrong.

"Selling that house was the best thing I have ever done in my life," the husband said. "I don't have to worry anymore if it might get wrecked in the next hurricane, whether the renters will trash the carpets, or about needing to cut the price to make sure it doesn't stand empty during peak season. And I don't have to write a check to the mortgage company every month that I never get back in rents."

Fortunately, those doctors were not wedded to a classic real estate fantasy: "I know I am losing money on this property every month, but I will make it all back and more, when I sell at a huge profit in a few years."

This expectation is directly in conflict with the research. Since the Second World War, the economic return of institutional real estate investments has been almost entirely a function of cash flow. Insurance companies, pension funds, and university endowments expect to earn a return on their real estate investments *based on the rental income stream, not on capital appreciation*.

If you own rental real estate, and you aren't getting paid cash every month, net of all costs, then you really haven't made a real estate *investment*. What you own is a *speculation*, with the possibility of a profit an implicit bet of the existence of a future buyer, even more optimistic than you, and willing to over-pay by an even larger margin than you did when you bought the property.

This is known as the "greater fool" theory of investing.

Three times in our careers, the real estate market has been so bad in New Jersey beach towns that real estate agents have refused to put *For Sale* signs in front of properties, hoping to conceal just how bad the resale markets had become. When we ask who bought the big houses right before the downturn, the answer is usually the same—doctors.

Every doctor who bought a beach house was confident that he would make money from his investment. All of them lost money on a cash flow basis. Their strategy for getting rich, in every case, required that a greater fool buy their money—losing property from them at a substantially higher price than they paid for it.

This strategy can work, but it requires an ever-increasing supply of greater fools. It is a strategy of hope and optimism, not of numbers and realism.

Strategy 2   Optimize savings

Optimizing savings means you should always direct your next savings dollar toward the highest *risk-adjusted after-tax* savings opportunity.

What does this mean? First, understand that a dollar of principal paid down against a debt may have every bit as much effect upon your net worth as a dollar saved to an investment account. *Debt paydown is a form of savings, and sometimes the most effective form*.

Your first priority should *always* be maximizing pre-tax savings to your employer retirement plan (401k, 403b, SEP, etc.). Those contributions will be withdrawn automatically from your paycheck, and your employer will often match a portion of your savings. This is "free money" in your account.

Let's examine why this type of savings is so effective, by looking at the after-tax consequence of directing $10,000 of income toward pre-tax vs. after-tax savings:

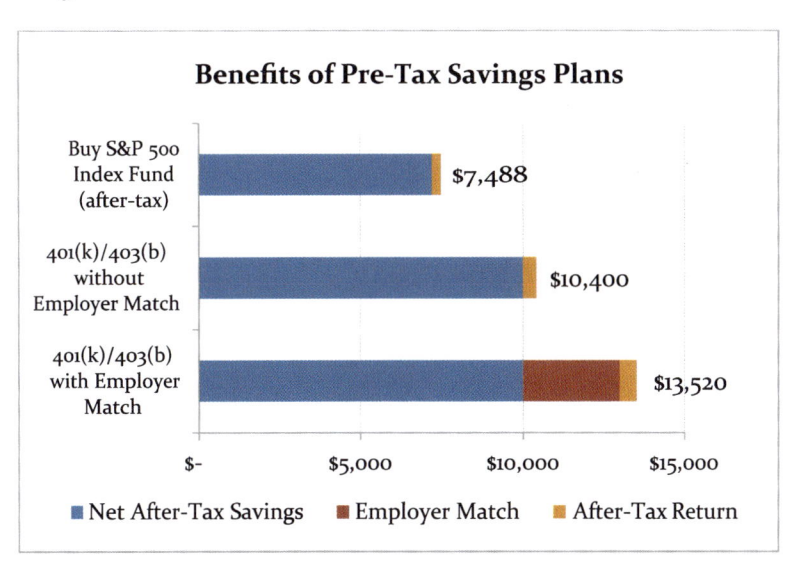

Benefits of Pre-Tax Savings Plans

Plan	Total
Buy S&P 500 Index Fund (after-tax)	$7,488
401(k)/403(b) without Employer Match	$10,400
401(k)/403(b) with Employer Match	$13,520

Legend: ■ Net After-Tax Savings   ■ Employer Match   ■ After-Tax Return

Because contributions are made pre-tax, and often matched by employers, the employer savings plan is very hard to beat.

For most of our physician clients, employer-based retirement savings plans have been the foundation of their financial independence, representing at their retirement the majority of their functional net worth. Those savings

46   Changing Outcomes

plan might be in the form of a 403(b) for doctors working for a non-profit hospital system, or of a 401(k) for those working for a for-profit hospital or medical practice. In some cases, salary deferral plans may be supplemented by a profit-sharing plan for the self-employed, or even (for a lucky few), by an actual pension benefit.

If you are committed to your financial turnaround strategy, we assume you have already maxed-out on your pre-tax employer savings opportunities, and recognize the need to save substantial additional dollars after-tax. Where should those savings go?

With both direct savings and debt paydown on an equal footing, you should direct your after-tax savings dollars toward the *highest risk-adjusted after-tax return*.[13]

Consider one set of possible choices:

➢ Pay down your home mortgage, with an interest rate of a tax-deductible 4.5%. (An after-tax cost of 3.2 %.)

➢ Buy a bank CD at a taxable 1.5%, with no market risk.

➢ Buy a stock index fund in a taxable account, with a projected return of 4% per year, with market risk.[14] (An implied after-tax return of 3.3%, assuming 18.8% tax rates on dividends and long-term capital gains.)

➢ Save to a 529 plan for a child who will enter college in three years. (Low-risk portfolio with a projected return of 1.25%, withdrawals for higher education tax-free.)

---

[13]The tax code gets ever more complex. Depending on income, the tax rate on dividends and long-term capital gains could be as low as 0% or as high as 23.8%. Your mortgage interest might be fully-deductible, or entirely non-deductible. The devil is in the details, and the nature of the tax devil changes frequently and capriciously. Hence the importance of the *principle* of after-tax return, rather than the specific sequence offered here.

[14]We believe this is a sensible projection of stock market returns, as of mid 2014, with the S&P 500 near all-time highs. The price of equity markets, and hence the projected return from owning stocks, can change dramatically over time. Again, this shows the importance of following the *principle* of after-tax return, rather than following simple advice such as, "Always pre-pay your home mortgage."

Here is a visual of this opportunity set:

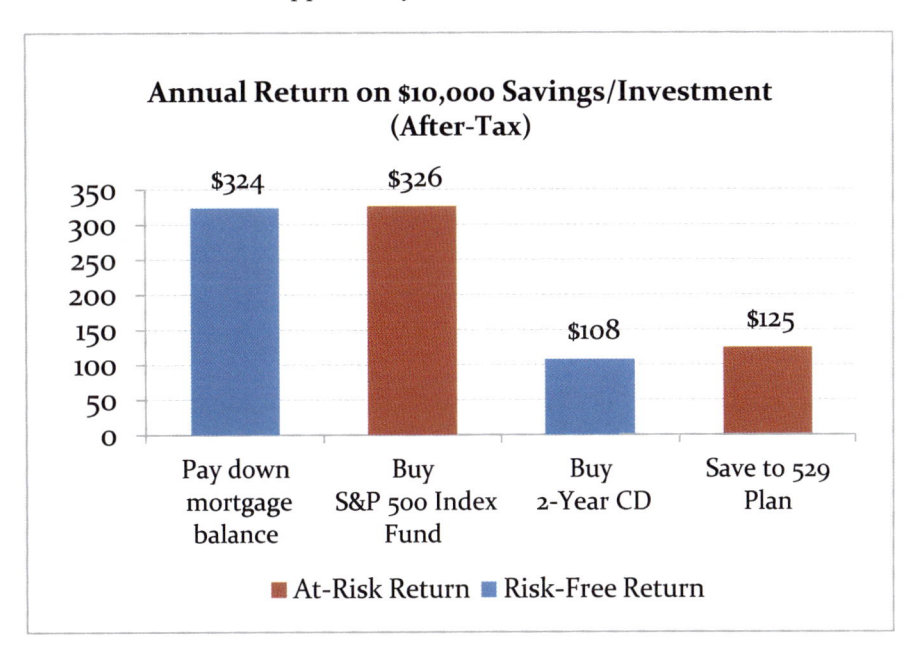

Annual Return on $10,000 Savings/Investment (After-Tax)

Option	Return
Pay down mortgage balance	$324 (Risk-Free)
Buy S&P 500 Index Fund	$326 (At-Risk)
Buy 2-Year CD	$108 (At-Risk)
Save to 529 Plan	$125 (At-Risk)

Based on the principle of highest after-tax, risk-adjusted return, the optimal sequence looks like this:

> - The stock index fund and the mortgage "pay" a similar after-tax return of just over 3.2%, but the return on mortgage paydown is risk-free, so paying down mortgage principal is the better choice.
> - The question of whether the 529 plan or S&P 500 Index Fund is better is difficult. In this case, the child is close to college, which means the 529 should be invested in lower-volatility assets, which offer both lower return and less risk.[15]

So 401k first, mortgage second, stock fund third, and 529 plan fourth.

The bank certificate, yielding just over 1% after-tax, will never yield a positive after-tax return, once adjusted for inflation. At best, it may provide

---

[15] If the child were younger and the period until she went to college longer, it would make sense to take more risk, and the choice might be between a taxable investment in the S&P 500 and a similar investment in the 529, which would be tax-free when withdrawn to pay college tuition. In that case, the 529 plan would be the better choice.

psychological comfort in a bear market. It can never make you rich. *The more you desire a low-volatility investment strategy, the more you will need to accumulate wealth by a brute force approach of massive savings.*

Keep in mind that this sequence is based upon a specific fact-pattern, at a specific point in time, under a specific tax regime. Given different interest rates, financial markets conditions, or tax rates, an entirely different sequence of savings might make more sense. But the *principle* would be unchanged—*always direct dollars to the highest risk-adjusted after-tax opportunity.*

Strategy 3   Pay yourself first, and make it automatic

There are two approaches to saving for your future. You can pay yourself last, or pay yourself first.

Paying yourself last is the default strategy for most Americans. "I'll be careful with money this month, and I'll take what I have left over and deposit it in my savings account, or open a Vanguard IRA, or send a check to my brokerage account."

Sometimes this works, for folks with plenty of time, modest spending habits, and lots of self-discipline. In other words, for very few actual human beings. It is easy to run out of money before you run out of month, and often that savings check never gets written.

The problem is actually compounded for high-income physicians with apparently bottomless checkbooks. If you write a $5,000 check to your investment account this month, is it enough? How much do you need to save? Will you remember every month?

A much better strategy is to *pay yourself first*. Make sure your monthly savings or debt payments happen automatically, before a single dollar makes its way into the accounts from which you manage your household and make discretionary purchases.

Our approach is to identify one account as the net-savings account, and direct a portion of each wage-earner's paycheck to this account by electronic funds transfer. From this account, we set up automatic semi-monthly or monthly transfers to other accounts based on priority. (It is usually better to fully pay down a higher-rate loan, and then begin accelerated paydown of the next loan, than to make partial extra principal payments to both.

By reducing your spending now, you improve your financial position in two ways. First, less spending means more savings, which should result in more wealth, which will in turn support higher cash flow in retirement. Second, by saving more you are growing used to spending less. In combination, *The Cliff* between the cash flow you spend while you are working and your potential post-retirement cash flow will be smaller.

Strategy 4   Manage discretionary spending

Pay yourself first. Make your savings automatic, and you will eliminate one of the primary drivers of over-consumption—the seemingly bottomless checkbook enjoyed by a peak-career specialist physician. It will not help to save automatically if your spending exceeds the rest of your net income.

Saving first is half the battle. The second half is managing spending.

Among the expenditures we've seen get physicians in trouble, the following are among the most common:

> Big houses
> Vacation properties, including "investment" properties that produce no investment return
> Family support
> Travel expenses
> Charitable contributions
> Expensive hobbies, such as boating or buying high-end autos

Real estate: We've already talked about the negative aspects of buying too much house. Owning your home is a wealth-building opportunity because it is a form of forced savings with specific tax advantages, *not* because houses reliably appreciate. The bigger the house, the higher the costs for upkeep, utilities and taxes, and the larger the drain on your long-term wealth. Even worse are vacation home that are carried at a negative cash flow. If you own a vacation property you rent out, and you don't cover your costs, what you are really doing is subsidizing other families' vacations.

Think back to Strategy 1. Do you have the opportunity to improve your net retirement savings by converting bad assets to good assets, either by down-sizing your home once your kids are gone, or by selling a money-losing "investment" property?

Family support: We all want to help our families, show respect to our parents, and make the going easier for our kids. But rescuing family members from economic calamity, often of their own making, can easily compromise your own financial security. Trying to help your cousin who just got downsized, your daughter and her husband who got in over their heads by buying too much house, or your son who is waiting tables in Manhattan while waiting for his big break as an actor, can represent an enormous drain on your finances just when you most need to maximize your savings.

Even worse, such economic outpatient care rarely alters the long-term financial trajectory of the person helped. Often, providing a "temporary" economic lifeline only delays the hour of reckoning. A year later, you may be out $50,000 or more, and the too-big house still ends up being repossessed after the divorce.

Vacations: Medicine is stressful, and vacations are a necessity not a luxury. But the *cost* of vacations is negotiable. A sensible way to manage travel expenses is with a three-year vacation plan. Decide how many weeks of vacation you will take each year. Examine the schedules of all your family members. Brainstorm about possible vacation destinations, keeping costs in mind. Then map out your travel three years in advance.

Simply being organized and purposeful about your time off should reduce your travel costs by roughly half, allowing you to take advantage of lower airfares, discounts on property rentals, and other cost savings. By booking early, you will also secure the best choices for everything. Often there is someone in the family with the combination of good computer skills and mild OCD ideal for booking bargain vacations.

Charity: We are great believers in giving back. We support several medical charities, and we do several charity bicycle rides every year. We are active in our church and synagogue. But we do not face the same pressures to donate as do our doctor clients.

In terms of your charitable activity, keep in mind that others think you are rich, while you (hopefully) recognize that you really aren't. Stepping up to the plate is expected of doctors in the context of their careers. We suggest that you make leadership-level donations only to projects that are closely linked to your work.

If you have achieved significant social status in three or more different charitable activities (i.e., your hospital's capital campaign, your medical school's annual fund, and through weekly pledges to your church or synagogue), you may be over-committed on the charity front. Also, keep in mind that a small amount of your time is worth a large amount of money. From a strictly economic perspective, it is usually better for you to write a check than to volunteer your time.

Charity can be a means for us to give back to our communities, in gratitude for the opportunities and blessings we have received. But as a physician, your charitable endeavors are unlikely to be your primary contribution to humanity. Your work as a doctor will be your biggest gift to the world.

Hobbies: There is an old cliché about owning a sailboat: "A sailboat is a hole in the water that you pour money into." This viewpoint can be extended to many expensive hobbies. You work hard, and you deserve to enjoy your life. Consider the total amount of satisfaction and relaxation you receive for the money you spend. *Are any of your hobbies providing low value per dollar spent?*

Several of our physician clients are active bicyclists. Recreational cycling is a good example of a high-value leisure activity. Many of our docs own awesome road bikes, in some cases costing up to $5,000 or even $10,000. But if that bike is kept for ten years, the monthly cost is less than $100, and cycling has profound health benefits. This is a relative bargain.

Compare that expense to owning a sailboat, where buying the boat itself only begins to describe the cost. On top of the purchase price, you have upkeep, storage, docking fees, and so on. Plus you have to factor in the time it takes to maintain it.

We know two doctors who own a winery, in a part of the country not known for excellent viticulture conditions. That is one heck of an expensive, and usually unprofitable, hobby.

Manage discretionary spending: Besides the large, structural cash drains discussed above, it is all too easy in our electronic-dollar world to cremate significant wealth through everyday spending that falls entirely below the threshold of conscious decision.

One effective way to manage your spending patterns is to establish a maximum dollar figure that you will spend without deliberate consideration. Determine a concrete dollar answer to each of the following questions:

- What will I buy without thinking twice?
- How much will I spend without consulting my spouse?
- What is my spending limit without checking with my accountant or financial advisor?

Here's a possible answer set:

- I will not spend more than $100 without sitting down for ten minutes to think about it.
- I won't spend $500 or more without talking to my spouse.
- I won't make any purchase or investment of $10,000 or more without speaking with one of my financial professionals.

54 Changing Outcomes

These dollar amounts are not set in stone. Find values that work for you. The principle is simply to think through the long-term benefit of any significant purchase, to make sure it will deliver fair value for dollar spent.

The purpose of managing spending is not to don a hair shirt, denying yourself necessities and luxuries. It is to mediate fairly between the necessities and luxuries you enjoy today, and those you will enjoy in the future, after retirement.

Strategy 5 Invest sensibly

"First, do no harm."
Hippocrates

Before offering a menu of investment strategies, let's establish three principles:

- Forget trying to out-perform the markets.
- Only own investments that have a price quoted in the public markets every business day.
- Decide on a sensible investment strategy and stick with it.

Let's examine the reasons behind each of our three rules.

Don't try to beat the markets. Given how our minds work, the investment "opportunity" that appears to have get-rich-quick potential is usually one that attaches to a recent record of out-performance. In 1999, the "hot" investment was technology stocks. In 2006, Las Vegas residential real estate. In 2010, gold.

All of these investments lost money. If purchased with leverage (borrowed money) in an attempt to multiply returns, an investor in any of these assets might have lost every dollar he put in.

You no longer have enough time to recover from investment errors. Your goal as a prudent investor should not be to *beat* the market, but simply to *capture* the market's return.

Only own liquid, publicly-traded securities that are priced every day. This means no real estate investments, no annuities or cash value life insurance, no limited partnerships, no private equity deals, no hedge funds.

By restricting yourself to publicly-traded securities, you immediately eliminate many financial disasters, including almost all investment scams, most investments with the potential for a total loss, and many of the deals where fees and costs will soak up a large part of your initial commitment of funds.[16]

---

[16] From Bernie Madoff to Banyan Partners, investment frauds and scams often share one selling point: the appeal of exclusivity. "This great opportunity isn't available to just anyone, but you can invest because you are smart/rich/connected/whatever." When you hear this pitch, run don't walk to the exit.

56   Changing Outcomes

What's left? A universe of tens of thousands of securities, including mutual funds, exchange-traded funds, low-cost index funds and individual stocks.

Choose one sensible strategy, and stick with it until you retire. This is tough to do, not least because no strategy offers a permanent advantage in the financial markets. No matter what approach you choose, there will be a point in the market cycle when you will be disappointed.

Difficult as it may be, you have to follow your plan doggedly, stubbornly, relentlessly, through good markets and bad, whether it is working or not. The alternative is switching strategies depending on what appears to be working right now, which almost inevitably fails.

What is a sensible investment strategy? We offer the following three options, in order of increasing complexity and (we believe) potential investment advantage.

These strategies are simple. As a non-professional investor, your first priority must always be to avoid irrecoverable errors. The simpler the strategy, the less likely you will get yourself in trouble by seeking an advantage.

Any of these options should work over time, but each of them will certainly under-perform during some part of the market cycle, and changing between them will almost inevitably lead to poor results:

1) Buy a target date fund with a scheduled maturity ten years beyond your intended retirement date.[17]

2) Follow a diversified investment strategy, with 50% or more of your assets in equities, using low-cost passive index funds. Here is a simple option that achieves meaningful diversification at low cost:

   a. 30% S&P 500 index fund

   b. 30% international stock index fund

   c. 20% Intermediate-term bond fund (municipal if purchased in a taxable account, high-quality corporate or government if purchased in a retirement account)

   d. 20% inflation-indexed Treasury fund

   e. Re-balance to this allocation once a year

---

[17]Better-educated individuals, particularly physicians, have a longer life expectancy than the average person. Since you are likely to live longer in retirement, your portfolio should be more growth-oriented than that of other retirees.

3) Invest in a diversified asset-allocation fund, tilted toward a value investment approach, and run by a manager with a solid long-term record. A good example is the Vanguard STAR Fund.

Which of these strategies do we follow for our clients? *None of the above.* In our practice, we implement a structured asset allocation process. We establish an optimized, diversified baseline portfolio, tilted toward value strategies, and systematically adjust our holdings to over-weight asset classes that are under-valued according to robust metrics.

We believe our strategy is prudent and potentially advantageous, but it is impractical for any individual to implement on his own, especially someone as busy as a practicing physician. This book is designed to focus on strategies you can implement yourself, not to serve as a solicitation for our investment services.

Given a choice between adequate savings and the promise of superior investment performance, always prioritize what you can control—your own savings rate. *No prudent, diversified investment strategy, including our own, can realistically make up for over-spending or under-saving.*

Strategy 6 Pray for rain

This is not so much as a strategy as a viewpoint. *Most investors completely misunderstand the economics of capital accumulation. They hope for the wrong things, and buy and sell at exactly the wrong times.*

The chart below shows the relationship between the U. S. stock market current price measured against inflation-adjusted trailing earnings, and the market's average annual return over the next ten years.

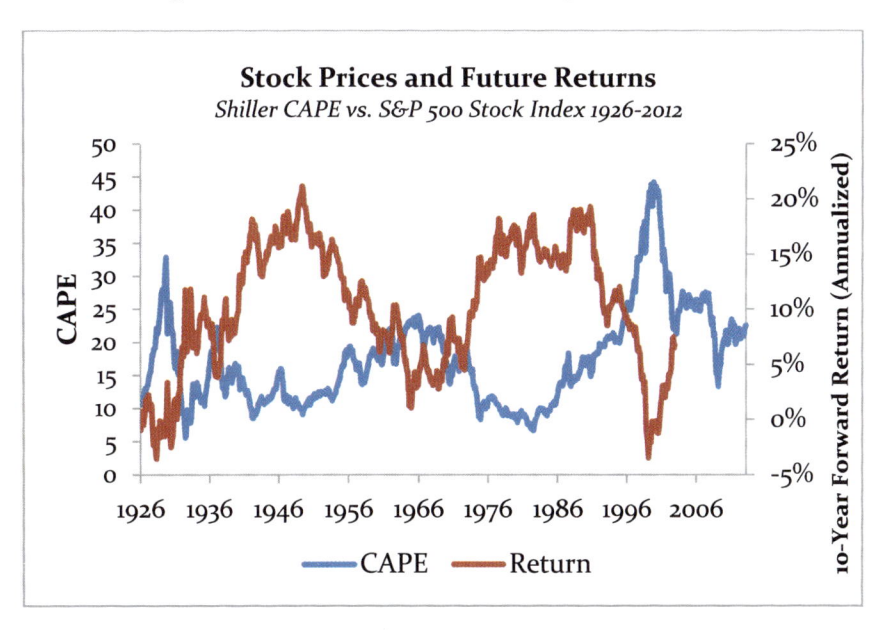

Stock Prices and Future Returns
Shiller CAPE vs. S&P 500 Stock Index 1926-2012

As you can see, there is a robust inverse correlation. This demonstrates a simple truth of investing—*when stock prices are high, future returns will be low, and when stock prices are low, future returns will be high.*[18]

Let's apply this principle in order to answer a simple question. *If you have ten or fifteen years until retirement, what should you wish for?*

The answer may surprise you. *You should wish for a bear market.*

---

[18] We are indebted to Yale economist Robert Shiller, author of the 1996 classic *Irrational Exuberance*, for both the concept of Cyclically-Adjusted Price Earnings and for the exhaustive data set, extending all the way back to 1871, that he makes publicly available on his web-site. Shiller shared the Nobel Prize in Economics with Eugene Fama in 2013.

If you are saving toward retirement, your ideal scenario is a stock market that declines continuously until the moment you retire, and then advances continuously for the rest of your life.

Obviously, this scenario—constant decline followed by constant advance—will not actually happen. But thinking clearly about the hypothetical can help you secure maximum advantage from the real-world opportunity set of investments you'll encounter in the future.

For the period until you retire—five years, ten years, fifteen years—you should be saving more each year than you spend. This means you will be a *net buyer* of investment assets. Whether buying tuna fish, a Mercedes sedan, an MRI machine, or an S&P 500 Index Fund, buyers always benefit from lower prices.

This book will be published in the second half of 2014. This year, the U. S. stock market hit a series of all-time highs. This is wonderful news for everyone who is already fully invested, and who is spending from and not saving to their portfolio. It can be discouraging for anyone who will be bringing new savings dollars to the table in the future.

But consider this: Since the Second World War, the U. S. stock market has declined by 10% or more about once a year, by 20% every three years, and by 30% or more once a decade. It is highly probable that, between now and your final retirement date, you will have several outstanding buying opportunities.

Markets go up and down. We can't control the *action* of the market, but we can control our *reactions*. The next time the stock market declines, be happy… and make sure you are a buyer.

Strategy 7 Make a gradual transition

Our grandparents' picture of retirement involved a gold watch after forty years of working for the same institution, a sudden shift from full-time work to full-time retirement, a pension, and life expectancy that meant less than a decade of actual retirement.

Those days are over.

Today's retirement can easily last three decades or longer, and the move from full-time work to full-time retirement can span a decade or more. As you consider your own retirement, picture a gradual transition, not an abrupt change.

Many physicians discount the value of working part-time, of no longer taking call, or of continuing to practice in an aspect of their specialty that is less highly-compensated.

Surely, the hourly compensation of a cardiac surgeon will be higher than that of a non-invasive cardiologist. If you work part-time, you will make less money than if you work full-time. But as we noted last chapter, the stock market is expensive, which is another way of saying that future returns may be low.

For an individual retiring at age 67, the sustainable cash flow from a diversified investment portfolio might be only 3%. This suggests that a $60,000 per year part-time income, for example as a hospitalist, will provide you sustainable cash flow comparable to an additional $2 million of investment assets.

As you work with your financial advisor to explore success strategies, calculate the effects on your lifetime finances of part-time work combined with a delayed full-retirement date. They will be larger than you think.

MONITORING

12   Taking Stock

"All progress begins with telling the truth."

Dan Sullivan
Founder, The Strategic Coach

To understand your financial position, you need to deal with both *subjective* factors and *objective* financial metrics. Either one without the other will cause a failure of proper *assessment* of your situation, which in turn will compromise the effectiveness of your financial *plan*.

Earlier in the book, we discussed some of the subjective, psychological challenges that keep most doctors from building walk-away wealth Now let's turn to some of the key objective measures needed to make an honest assessment of your present situation.

As a physician, you are trained to gather and evaluate data. You might be a pediatrician, trying to understand the reason for a teenage girl's weight loss. You might be a pulmonologist, working to determine the cause of a persistent cough, or a cardiologist treating a middle-aged businessman with chest pains. When you see a new patient, often one of the first things you will do is order tests, to help you make an accurate diagnosis and design an effective treatment plan.

Data is equally important in a successful financial turnaround strategy. What can we learn from your financial test results?

- ➢ What is your income? Your effective tax rate? What is your after-tax income?

- ➢ Do you fully qualify (maximize) your pre-tax employer savings plans? Does your employer make or match contributions?

- ➢ What is your annual savings rate, as a percentage of your pre-tax income?

- ➢ What are your productive assets? Your unproductive assets? What is your functional net worth, compared to your income? Compared to other physicians? Compared to the typical high earner who is not a physician? Compared to what you will need to retire without cutting spending?

- Do you have any outstanding consumer debts? Business debts? Mortgages? Have you co-signed any loans? What are the terms and interest rates of each debt?
- Is anyone dependent on you? Will you receive an inheritance?
- Will you receive a pension? Is it fully vested? Will you have a lump-sum alternative?
- Finally, and crucially, when do you plan to retire? How much after-tax income do you wish to spend each month?

Each of these measures is important, and your accountant and financial advisor will need to understand them. But these are too many variables for you to monitor yourself on an ongoing basis. To place yourself in a stronger financial position, we suggest that you focus on tracking two measures:

- Net effective savings
- Functional net worth

These will be the primary drivers of your wealth accumulation over the next ten years.

13 Finding the Right Advisor

"There are two ways to acquire wisdom. You can buy it, or you can rent it."

Benjamin Franklin

If you've never worked with an advisor before, and you find yourself far from your goals, it may be time to get your ego and your need for control out of the way of your financial security, and to find the right advisor.

If you are already working with an advisor, but still falling short, you need to figure out what isn't working:

- Is he the wrong advisor, or are you a non-compliant patient?
- Is he communicating the wrong things, or are you not listening?
- Are you saving too little and spending too much?
- Are you and your advisor implementing an effective investment strategy?

In choosing an advisor, you need someone who is not intimidated by the MD or DO after your name, someone who is more committed to your lifetime financial security than to your short-term psychological comfort, who will tell you the truth even if it hurts, and who will push you to make the right decisions even when financial markets get scary.

Your advisor's first job is to understand you, your current situation, and where you want to go—both objective factors like net worth, tax bracket, and income, as well as subjective factors like risk tolerance, family money dynamics, and aspirations.

Your advisor's second job is to develop a *realistic* recovery plan. This should be a serious, written, documented financial analysis. In terms of the technical aspects, it should include both a linear and a Monte Carlo analysis of cash flow in retirement. Your plan should be shared with all of the members of your advisory team, including your accountant, attorney, and perhaps even your practice manager.

This plan is the road map for your financial recovery. It must be real, compelling, and convincing. If it isn't, you will not follow it.

Making the changes of habit, lifestyle, and outlook necessary to get your finances on track will be one of the hardest things you ever do in your life.

We say that fully aware of how difficult it is to secure admission to medical school, how challenging to complete a course of medical education, and how exhausting to survive residency and fellowship.

If you are going to make the very difficult changes needed to get your finances back on track, you need a success strategy you can believe in. *You must be confident that your sacrifices of present lifestyle for future financial security will be rewarded.*

14   Negotiating with Yourself

"I asked myself, what's the most important organ in the body? Why the brain, of course. Then I thought, wait a minute. Who's telling me this?"

Comedian Emo Phillips

Creating a financial recovery plan is an iterative process. We start with realistic assumptions, accurate financial data, and a target income goal in retirement. We develop a baseline strategy, and then begin to evaluate the moving parts. This process involves a series of tradeoffs:

- How much are you willing to cut spending now to enjoy more cash flow in retirement?
- Do you have a vacation property that you rarely use, that could be sold and reinvested in economically productive assets?
- Do you want or need to retire earlier, even if it means less cash flow?
- Might you be willing to work longer than you planned, if the benefit is greater confidence you can live the life you want in retirement?

As you explore these alternatives, your unconscious thought process may sound like this: "If I save more money, as this advisor suggests, I will have much less cash flow to purchase goods, services and experiences I really enjoy. I will miss out on all those cool things, just so my advisor can make more money running my portfolio. How is that fun?"

In reality, you are not negotiating with your financial advisor, but with yourself: "Doctor Jones version 2014, may I introduce you to Doctor Jones version 2025?"

Your advisor may be sitting on the other side of the table, but she is not really a party to the negotiation. At the end of the day, your financial advisor does not have a dog in this fight. If you don't build enough capital, it will have small effect on that advisor's lifestyle. It could ruin yours.

As you engage in this inter-generational dialogue with yourself, make sure you negotiate in good faith. *Do not make the mistake of believing your future self will value different activities or want to live a different lifestyle than you enjoy today.*

We have worked with hundreds of retirees over more than three decades in practice. The retired folks we know have not taken to their rockers. They are skiing, cycling, traveling the world, driving RVs cross country, consulting, visiting kids and grandkids, attending the theater, dining out, reading (and writing) books.

Trust us. When you reach age 70, 80, even 90, expect yourself to be active, mentally sharp, and engaged with the world. You will need money to live the life you want, exactly as you need it today.

Treat your future self as you would treat a patient or a valued colleague—with attention, compassion, and respect.

15 Keeping Score

"A goal without a measure is just a wish."

Japanese business maxim

As you begin your financial recovery, it can be hard to stay on track. You will need to change your conceptual scorecard from one that focuses on relative social status to one based on your own personal and specific financial goals.

It may help if you consider yourself a potentially non-compliant patient, like a diabetic who eats dessert five nights a week, or a harried executive with high cholesterol who won't take his statins or cut back on the cheeseburgers.

Remember, the two key measurables for you to track are *net effective savings* and *functional net worth*. Here are the graphics we use to track these for our clients:

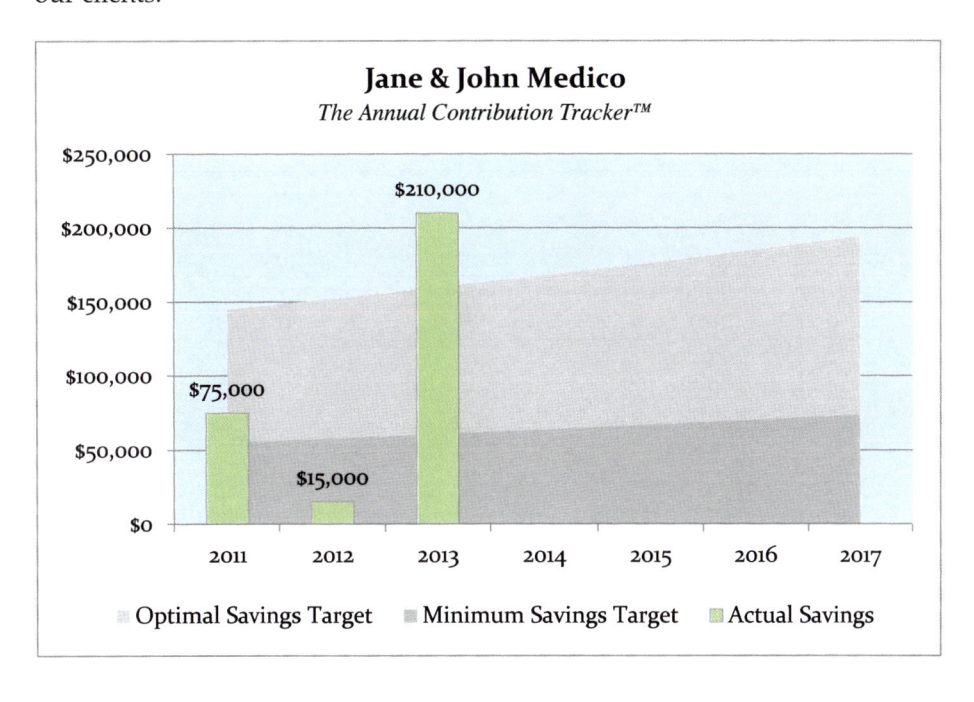

Jane & John Medico
The Annual Contribution Tracker™

[Bar chart showing Actual Savings: $75,000 (2011), $15,000 (2012), $210,000 (2013), with Optimal Savings Target and Minimum Savings Target bands across 2011–2017]

72 Changing Outcomes

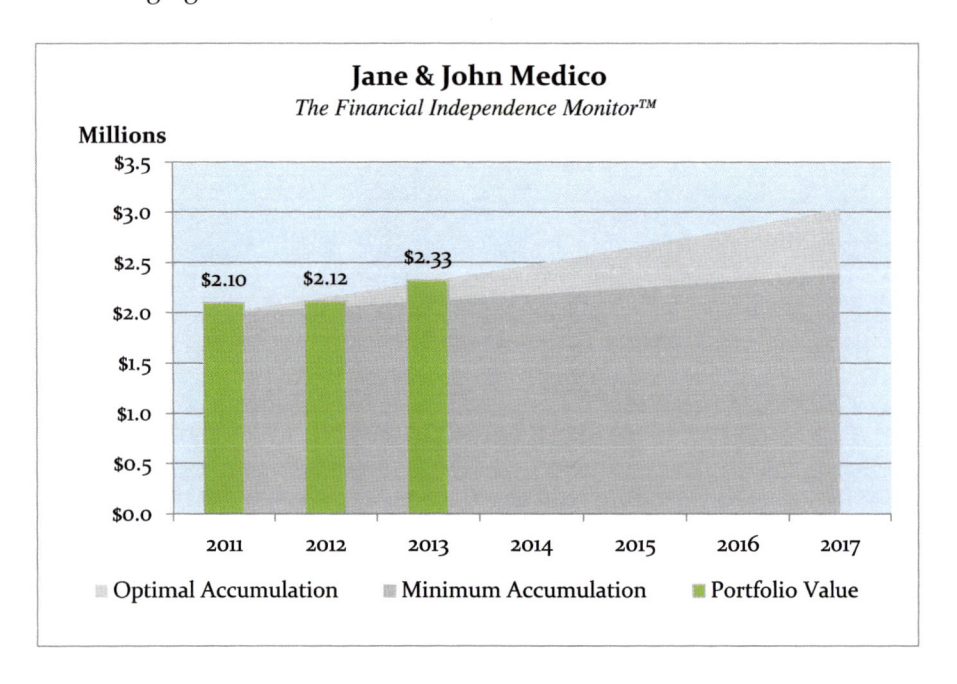

Jane & John Medico
The Financial Independence Monitor™

[Chart showing Millions on y-axis ($0.0 to $3.5) and years 2011-2017 on x-axis. Green bars (Portfolio Value): 2011 = $2.10, 2012 = $2.12, 2013 = $2.33. Legend: Optimal Accumulation, Minimum Accumulation, Portfolio Value.]

Note that both graphics track actual savings and/or accumulation against *two* targets. The lower target is what you will need to retire with a minimum acceptable standard of living. The higher target is what is needed to retire, preserving both capital and income in the face of inflation, for the rest of your life. (We call this the "live forever" target.)

We find this "two-targets" approach helps encourage constructive savings habits. Tracking against only a *minimum* goal encourages just-good-enough savings rates in the good years, and shortfalls during more economically difficult periods. The practical result is insufficient savings and hence inadequate capital formation.

On the other hand, tracking against only the *optimal* goal can be downright discouraging. Why save at all if you are doomed to always fall short?

The combination provides both conceptual context and psychological support for an aggressive savings strategy, much as providing a healthy range for HDL cholesterol can help put the results of a lipids screen in context.

Save even the minimum, and you should accumulate more assets than 95% of all Americans, including most of your physician peers. Save the optimal amount, and you will make yourself as financially bulletproof as it is possible to be, in our modern, volatile and constantly-changing financial landscape.

OUTCOMES

16 Working the Plan

"The journey of a thousand miles begins with a single step."
                                                               Lao Tzu

Let's re-visit Jane and John Medico, the fictional doctors we met early in the book, and use them to illustrate the potential benefits of our seven financial turnaround strategies. On the next two pages, we've provided a five-year income projection and a before-and-after functional balance sheet, showing the potential benefits of making the following changes:

1) Retire credit-card debt.

2) Sell the vacation property, the rental income from which falls far short of the annual debt service, maintenance and tax costs.

3) Sell the timeshare, which also has annual maintenance costs and which the Medicos do not currently use.

4) Invest the net proceeds from sale of the properties, and the extra yearly cash flow freed up from debt service, in investment assets.

5) When one of the Medico's children graduates from college in the second plan year, invest the cash flow freed up from tuition instead of spending it.

6) Adopt a five-year vacation plan, targeting total vacation spending of less than 5% of pre-tax income, and put that plan in place over three years.

As you can see, the potential benefits of re-directing money from dead assets to functional assets, and of beginning to control discretionary spending, are profound.

Jane & John Medico
Income Statement

	Year 1	Year 2	Year 3	Year 4	Year 5
Income:					
Annual salary	$ 700,000	$ 700,000	$ 700,000	$ 700,000	$ 700,000
Contribution to 401k	$ 45,000	$ 45,000	$ 45,000	$ 45,000	$ 45,000
Taxable salary	$ 655,000	$ 655,000	$ 655,000	$ 655,000	$ 655,000
Income taxes	$ 183,400	$ 183,400	$ 183,400	$ 183,400	$ 183,400
After-tax cash flow	$ 471,600	$ 471,600	$ 471,600	$ 471,600	$ 471,600
Expenses:					
Benefits costs	$ (15,000)	$ (15,000)	$ (15,000)	$ (15,000)	$ (15,000)
Debt service	$ (71,851)	$ (23,419)	$ (23,245)	$ (23,038)	$ (22,807)
Annual upkeep on real property	$ (149,500)	$ (49,500)	$ (49,500)	$ (49,500)	$ (49,500)
Travel	$ (50,000)	$ (40,000)	$ (30,000)	$ (30,000)	$ (30,000)
Education costs	$ (110,000)	$ (110,000)	$ (30,000)	$ (30,000)	$ (30,000)
Household expenses	$ (70,000)	$ (70,000)	$ (70,000)	$ (70,000)	$ (70,000)
Cash flow from assets sold	$ -	$ 225,000			
Free cash flow	$ 5,249	$ 388,681	$ 253,855	$ 254,062	$ 254,293
Addition to taxable investments	$ -	$ 370,000	$ 230,000	$ 230,000	$ 230,000

Jane & John Medico
Balance Sheet

	Year 1	Year 2	Year 3	Year 4	Year 5
Assets					
Checking accounts	$100,000	$105,249	$123,930	$147,785	$171,847
Certificates of Deposit	$25,000	$25,375	$25,756	$26,142	$26,534
401k plans	$450,000	$495,000	$540,000	$585,000	$630,000
Long-term taxable growth investments	$0	$370,000	$618,500	$879,425	$1,153,396
Principal residence	$825,000	$825,000	$825,000	$825,000	$825,000
Vacation property	$1,250,000	$0	$0	$0	$0
Time share	$50,000	$0	$0	$0	$0
Automobiles	$100,000	$90,000	$81,000	$72,900	$65,610
Personal property	$250,000	$250,000	$250,000	$250,000	$250,000
Artwork	$150,000	$150,000	$150,000	$150,000	$150,000
Total assets	$3,200,000	$2,310,624	$2,614,186	$2,936,252	$3,272,387
Functional assets	$575,000	$995,624	$1,308,186	$1,638,352	$1,981,777
Liabilities					
Mortgage on principal residence	$550,000	$541,750	$533,624	$525,619	$517,735
Mortgage on vacation property	$900,000	$0	$0	$0	$0
Auto loans	$60,000	$48,000	$38,400	$30,720	$24,576
Credit cards	$10,000	$0	$0	$0	$0
Total liabilities	$1,520,000	$589,750	$572,024	$556,339	$542,311
Net Worth	$1,680,000	$1,720,874	$2,042,162	$2,379,913	$2,730,076
Functional Net Worth	($945,000)	$405,874	$736,162	$1,082,013	$1,439,466

Physician Profile: Second Acts

"There are no second acts in American lives."
                                                F. Scott Fitzgerald

Scott Fitzgerald was wrong about second acts. As proof, I offer Dr. Jack McConnell, who I was privileged to meet in the early 2000s.

McConnell served in the Navy after medical school, where he contracted tuberculosis and was confined to bed for a year. Once recovered, he opened his own practice in New Orleans, but was soon hired by a pharmaceutical company to do research. One of his first projects was finding a more effective diagnosis for the tuberculosis from which he'd suffered. He found an effective test, developed by a horse doctor, commercialized it, and soon it was marketed worldwide. That tuberculin tine test is still used today.

In the 1960s, he directed the development and testing of acetaminophen for pain relief. The uncoated pills were incredibly bitter, so he went into the lab immediately before FDA approval and re-formulated the tablets to make them more palatable. "You could never do that today," he commented when I met him. That drug was marketed as Tylenol.

In the 1980s, working as director of advanced technology for Johnson & Johnson, he directed the team that developed the first MRI system. In the late 1980s, near retirement, he helped pass the bills that created the Human Genome Project, and served as a trustee for the Institute for Genomic Research.

In 1989, McConnell retired to Hilton Head, South Carolina, expecting to play golf. But he soon became involved in another project-the delivery of health care to indigent patients. His new project became known as Volunteers in Medicine. He got the state legislature to pass laws creating special licenses for retired health care professionals practicing in free clinics, obtained malpractice insurance from the state medical association, and opened the first Volunteers in Medicine clinic in 1994.

Today that clinic treats thousands of people each year, and is estimated to save local doctors and hospitals $5 million each year in what would otherwise be uncompensated medical care. McConnell created a foundation to help groups start clinics in other states. Today there are almost 100 Volunteers in Medicine clinics in 29 states.

80   Changing Outcomes

The original clinic's mission statement reads:

May we have eyes to see those rendered invisible and excluded, open arms and hearts to reach out and include them, healing hands to touch their lives with love, and in the process, heal ourselves.

McConnell made a great point in an interview a few years back: "You don't quit being a doctor when you retire."

Contemplating everything McConnell has accomplished so far in his life is overwhelming. But thinking about what you have to contribute over the next thirty years of your own life should be inspiring.

—JSH

17   Your Bigger Future

"It is neither wealth nor splendor; but tranquility and occupation which give you happiness."

Thomas Jefferson

We are going to share an exercise created by Dan Sullivan of *The Strategic Coach*, called *The Bigger Future*.

Take a legal pad, draw a vertical line down the center, and another line across the page near the top. Above the line on the left, write *The Set Up*, and below it write the next ten-year period. (Right now, that would be 2014-2024.) Above the right line, write *The Bigger Future*, and the dates of the ten years following. (Today, 2024-2034.)

The first period, the next ten years, is when you will accomplish a variety of objectives, personal and professional, designed to get you ready for the following phase of your life. That second period, the one you have labeled *The Bigger Future*, is when you will accomplish the most important results of your entire lifetime.[19]

Here is our one rule: *None of the elements of your* Bigger Future *should rely on your above-average physician's income to pursue.* So 'Own a house in the South of France' does not qualify, but 'Ride my bicycle across the United States' does. So does 'Publish a book,' 'Go fishing with my grandson,' or 'Learn to speak Italian.'

The purpose of this exercise is to generate optimism and excitement about your future. That positive energy can help drive the changes needed to power your financial recovery.

During your working years, you have been chronically short of time and subject to high levels of stress. Often, your time off has reflected a need for recovery, more than a pursuit of experience.

---

[19]If you won the Nobel Prize in Physiology and Medicine based on work you did before age 30, this may seem like a ridiculous metric. How can you top that? What we suggest is that you adopt an alternative measurement metric, within which you can accomplish new and great things. Instead of focusing on your career, make a breakthrough in your relationships, or accomplish an athletic challenge, or write that novel you've been thinking about for years. (One of our cardiologist clients has already published three murder mysteries, all set in the framework of a large-hospital.)

Once retired, or as you begin the gradual transition process from full-time work to full-time retirement, you will for the first time in decades begin to have the time and the energy to contemplate making different choices.

As you approach retirement, our advice is to *choose experiences over possessions*.

18 A Life Well Lived

"We must never forget that practicing medicine is a privilege."
Chief of Cardiology
Midwestern teaching hospital

Despite a general collapse of trust in American institutions, including journalism, higher education, government, and business, doctors continue to command the public's trust like no other profession.

The economics of medicine have taken a beating in recent years. But even though our nation faces continuing challenges in how we provide health care, how we pay for it, and how we compensate our physicians, we continue to create most of the innovations in medical care for the entire world.

The hope of better health offered by the American healthcare system and the physicians who staff it remains very real, and doctors continue to soldier bravely on, serving their patients with determination and skill.

More than anything else, writing our two books for doctors has made us appreciate, more than ever, the lifelong sacrifices that physicians make for the benefit of their patients. Thank you for all you do.

Afterword

In this little book, we have outlined a recovery strategy for peak-career physicians planning to retire within fifteen years. We hope we have left you with renewed optimism about your ability to build lifetime financial security.

- If you have any suggestions about how this guide could be improved, please email us at feedback@tgsfin.com.
- If you would like information about our fee-based advisory programs for physicians, email us at questions@tgsfin.com, or go to the *Triage* web-site at www.triage-md.com.
- If you would like to schedule an initial consultation with one of our financial advisors, please call us at (800) 525-4075.

Since the founding of TGS Financial Advisors in 1990, helping physicians achieve better financial outcomes has been a key focus of our independent advisory practice. If you wish to explore how we can help you manage your finances today, to help you create better choices years from now, we would welcome the opportunity to meet with you.

About the Authors

David A. Burd, CFP®
A graduate of Swarthmore College, David has worked in the investment field since 1978. He holds the CERTIFIED FINANCIAL PLANNER™ certification. He co-founded TGS Financial Advisors with Jim Hemphill in 1990.

David's practice concentrates on the financial needs of physicians and medical specialists. David was named as one of *The Best Financial Advisers for Doctors* by *Medical Economics* magazine in 2006, 2010, 2011, 2012, and 2013.

David is married to Charlene, who has a Master's in Education and is a counselor in the Delran Middle School in New Jersey. They have two children, Zachary and Samantha. They live in Voorhees, New Jersey.

James S. Hemphill, CFP®, CIMA
Jim graduated from Swarthmore College. He has been managing investment portfolios since 1978. He co-founded TGS Financial Advisors with David Burd in 1990.

Jim holds the CERTIFIED FINANCIAL PLANNER™, and Certified Investment Management Analyst certifications.

Jim's practice focuses on successfully managing the retirement transition, especially for successful entrepreneurs selling a business. He serves as the firm's *Chief Investment Strategist*. For his up to date thoughts on the markets and investment strategy, visit his blog, *The Glass Half Full*.

Jim is married to Amy, who received her Master of Public Health from Johns Hopkins University in 1998. They have two sons, Jack and Alex, and a daughter, Katharine. They live in West Chester, Pennsylvania.

Made in the USA
San Bernardino, CA
29 September 2014